IT'S TIME TO LEARN ABOUT ARMADILLOS

It's Time to Learn about Armadillos

Walter the Educator

Silent King Books
A WhichHead Entertainment Imprint

Copyright © 2025 by Walter the Educator

All rights reserved. No part of this book may be reproduced in any manner whatsoever without written per- mission except in the case of brief quotations embodied in critical articles and reviews.

First Printing, 2024

Disclaimer

This book is a literary work; the story is not about specific persons, locations, situations, and/or circumstances unless mentioned in a historical context. Any resemblance to real persons, locations, situations, and/or circumstances is coincidental. This book is for entertainment and informational purposes only. The author and publisher offer this information without warranties expressed or implied. No matter the grounds, neither the author nor the publisher will be accountable for any losses, injuries, or other damages caused by the reader's use of this book. The use of this book acknowledges an understanding and acceptance of this disclaimer.

It's Time to Learn about Armadillos is a collectible early learning book by Walter the Educator suitable for all ages belonging to Walter the Educator's Time to Eat Book Series. Collect more books at WaltertheEducator.com

USE THE EXTRA SPACE TO TAKE NOTES AND DOCUMENT YOUR MEMORIES

ARMADILLOS

In warm, wide lands where grasses grow,

It's Time to Learn about
Armadillos

A creature small walks nice and slow.

With armored plates from head to toe,

It's an armadillo, don't you know?

Its shell is hard, its body round,

It scurries softly on the ground.

With tiny claws so sharp and neat,

It digs for food beneath its feet.

It loves to snack on bugs so small,

Like ants and worms, it eats them all!

With a tongue so long and quick to flick,

It grabs its meal and slurps it slick!

Some armadillos roll up tight,

A little ball, a funny sight!

When danger's near, they do not fight,

They curl up safe and hold on tight.

It's Time to Learn about
Armadillos

With noses keen and ears so wide,

They sniff and listen, then they hide.

They dig deep burrows underground,

Where they are safe and sleep so sound.

Their legs are short, but they can run,

Through grass and dirt, they dash for fun!

They may look slow, but don't be fooled,

They zip away when they are schooled!

Some are tiny, pink, and bright,

Some are big and strong with might.

From giant kinds to ones so small,

Armadillos wow us all!

They cannot see so well, it's true,

But smell and sound will help them through.

They know just when to dig or dash,

It's Time to Learn about
Armadillos

Before a predator can crash!

At night they roam, by day they rest,

Inside their burrows, safe and best.

When stars come out, they start to creep,

And look for food before they sleep.

So if you see this armored friend,

Just watch it waddle, don't pretend!

It may be shy, it may be small,

It's Time to Learn about
Armadillos

But armadillos charm us all!

ABOUT THE CREATOR

Walter the Educator is one of the pseudonyms for Walter Anderson. Formally educated in Chemistry, Business, and Education, he is an educator, an author, a diverse entrepreneur, and he is the son of a disabled war veteran. "Walter the Educator" shares his time between educating and creating. He holds interests and owns several creative projects that entertain, enlighten, enhance, and educate, hoping to inspire and motivate you. Follow, find new works, and stay up to date with Walter the Educator™

at WaltertheEducator.com

www.ingramcontent.com/pod-product-compliance
Lightning Source LLC
LaVergne TN
LVHW052017060526
838201LV00059B/4069